Head Lice

Allison Lassieur

My Health

Franklin Watts

A Division of Grolier Publishing

New York • London • Hong Kong • Sydney

Danbury, Connecticut

Photographs ©: Custom Medical Stock Photo: 10, 42; Nance S. Trueworthy: 4, 21, 31, 32, 38; Peter Arnold Inc.: 12 (David Scharf); Photo Researchers: 7 (Biophoto Associates), 9 top right (Vaughan Fleming/SPL), 11, 27 right (Christian Gautier/Jacana), 14 (ST. Bartholomew's Hospital/SPL), 19 (Oliver Meckes), 25 (Gary Retherford), PhotoEdit: 29 (Tony Freeman), 15 right (Michael Newman), 15 left, 20, 34, 40 (D. Young-Wolff); Superstock, Inc.: 17; Tony Stone Images: 9 top left (Robert Brons), 8 (Tim Flach); Visuals Unlimited: 9 bottom (Glenn M. Oliver), 27 left (A. M. Siegelman), 35 (Steve Strickland); William E. Ferguson, Ph.D: 5, 41.

Cartoons by Rick Stromoski

Visit Franklin Watts on the Internet at:
http://publishing.grolier.com

Library of Congress Cataloging-in-Publication Data

Lassieur, Allison.
    Head Lice / by Allison Lassieur
        p. cm.—(My Health)
    Includes bibliographical references and index.
    Summary: Describes the physical features, behavior, and life cycle of head lice, compares them to body lice, and explains how to get rid of them.
    ISBN 0-531-11624-7 (lib. bdg.)   0-531-16450-0 (pbk.)
    1. Pediculosis—Juvenile literature. [1. Pediculosis. 2. Lice.]
I. Title. II. Series.
RL764.P4L37   1999
616.5'7—dc21   98-53649
                                            CIP
                                            AC

GROLIER
PUBLISHING

Cntents

I've Got Critters on My Head

Your head itches. Scratch, scratch. Maybe you tell your teacher. You might let your mom or dad know. One of them takes a look at your head. Most of the time an itchy head is nothing to worry about. Sometimes, though, it is a sign that head lice have found a home in your hair!

Head lice are tiny insects that live on human heads. They look grayish white. Adult lice are about the size of sesame seeds. These creepy crawlies aren't like other insects. They don't have wings, so they can't fly. They can't jump either. All they can do is crawl.

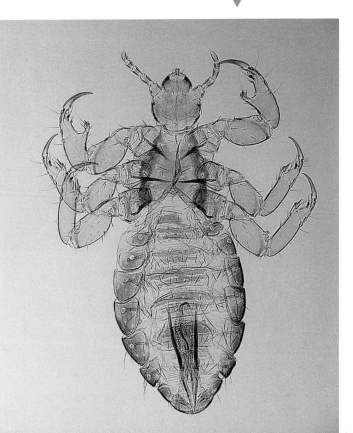

◄ One sign that you may have head lice is an itchy head.

Having a head full of lice sounds horrible. Who wants insects in their hair? But having head lice really isn't too serious. Lice can be annoying, but they don't usually make you sick.

If you find out you have head lice, don't panic. You're not alone. Other kids in your school probably have them too. Humans have been pestered by these pests for thousands of years. What exactly are head lice? Turn the page to find out more.

Did You Know...

Anyone with hair can get lice, no matter who he or she is or where he or she lives. Scientists have found lice on mummies— showing that even ancient people were bugged by lice! In fact, ancient Egyptians shaved their heads to keep lice away.

What Is a Louse?

Head lice are **ectoparasites**. That's a mouthful! *Ecto-* means "outside." **Parasites** are creatures that live and feed on other living things. So an ectoparasite is an animal that lives and feeds on the outside of another animal.

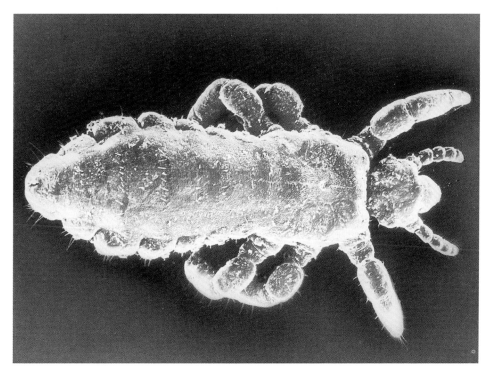

Most lice feed on blood every 3 to 6 hours.

Why Does Your Head Itch?

A louse's huge claws are great for grasping hair.

Lice use their strong claws to hang onto your hair. They need to hold on tight when they feed on your blood! Lice have special mouthparts made for sucking blood. When a louse feels hungry, it bites your skin for a drop of dinner.

The louse leaves a tiny bit of spit in the skin as it feeds. That's what causes the itchy feeling on your head. Sometimes it might cause a rash. Most of the time, though, it just makes you scratch.

Many insect ectoparasites use humans for food. Ticks, chiggers, leeches, and even some flies are ectoparasites. They think human blood tastes great. Head lice think so too.

Head lice like human scalps best. That's usually the only part of your body they live on. They hatch, live, eat, and die without ever leaving your scalp!

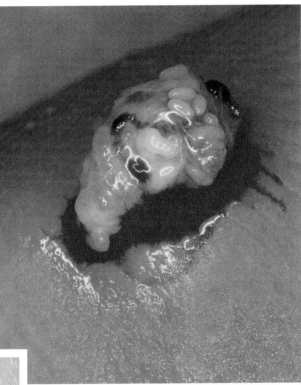

A tick (top left) uses small barbs in its mouth area to puncture skin. This chigger (top right) and its eggs have been squeezed out of skin on a foot. Leeches (bottom) live in fresh water, such as lakes or ponds.

Lice have three stages in their lives: egg, **nymph**, and adult. Adult female lice lay their eggs on strands of hair. The eggs are called **nits.** Nits look like tiny white flakes on your hair. But these flakes don't come off easily! A strong gummy substance makes them stick to hair.

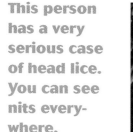

This person has a very serious case of head lice. You can see nits everywhere.

After about a week, young lice hatch out of the nits. These tiny critters are called nymphs. A newly hatched nymph is clear, but it turns reddish brown after eating its first meal of blood. Nymphs have the same shape as adult lice, but they are smaller. A nymph does just two things—it eats and sheds its special skin called an **exoskeleton**. Every nymph sheds its exoskeleton three times as it grows. It takes about 10 days for a nymph to become an adult. After a nymph sheds its skin the third time, it is officially grown up.

As soon as a female louse becomes an adult, it starts laying nits. It lays four to six nits every day until it dies about a month later. A female may lay as many as 200 eggs in its lifetime. That's a busy louse!

This louse has just laid a nit. In about 10 days, the nit will hatch and a nymph will pop out.

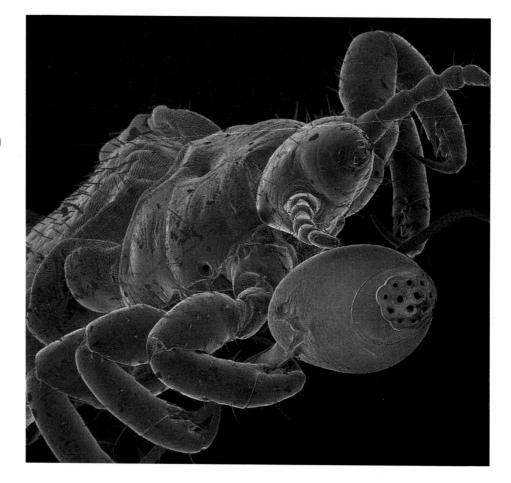

Activity 1: Counting Nits

How fast can a female produce a huge family of lice? Tear a sheet of paper into many small pieces. Lay one piece on a table. It stands for the female louse.

Let's say that the female lays five nits a day. How many nits are there after 1 day? Place a piece of paper on the table to represent each nit. How many nits are there after 3 days? By now, there are a lot of pieces of paper on the table! How many nits will there be after 1 month, or 30 days? Don't forget that after 10 days, the female young begin to lay nits of their own.

Where did all these lice come from? Why did they decide to live on *your* head? Turn the page to find out how people get lice.

How You Get Lice

If someone you know has lice, adults around you might start to panic. They don't want the lice to spread to you. But lice can't jump or fly. They can't even crawl very far. The lice don't want to leave the head they live on. They like their warm home! So how do they spread so fast?

If you look closely at this photo, you will see many nits and one adult louse.

Lots of things can shake up a louse's world. Sometimes lice get yanked out of a person's hair by a comb or a brush. If the person rubs his or her head with a towel after taking a shower, the lice might come loose. Hair bands, hair clips, and ponytail holders can snag these tiny critters. Sometimes lice let go of a hair shaft and fall into baseball caps, shirts, and scarves. If

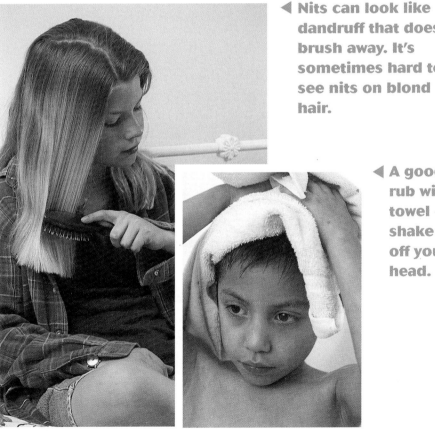

◀ Nits can look like dandruff that doesn't brush away. It's sometimes hard to see nits on blond hair.

◀ A good rub with a towel can shake lice off your head.

two heads are close together, a louse might just crawl from one head to another. For such small insects, lice can move fast.

Sharing combs, brushes, hats or other clothing, or even pillows and sheets is another way for lice to spread. If an object with lice on it touches your head, there's a chance that you'll get lice, too.

When you're outside playing sports, catching lice is probably the last thing on your mind. But sharing sports helmets is also one way for lice to move from person to person.

Did You Know...

Girls are more likely to get lice than boys. African-Americans hardly ever get lice.

Children at an elementary school in Fairfax County, Virginia, just couldn't get rid of their lice. In this case, most of the children who had lice were boys. Even after all the boys were treated, the lice kept coming back. Then someone remembered that all the boys played baseball together. It turned out that every per-

Get That Helmet Clean

It's a good idea to keep your sports helmet clean. Lice hate a clean helmet! Cleaning it out is easy, but you may need an adult to help you.

1. Take out any foam padding inside the helmet. This padding is usually attached with Velcro, so it should come out easily.

2. Clean the inside of the helmet with a small hand-held vacuum. Wipe hard-to-reach places with a cloth. Vacuum the foam padding too.

3. Wrap the helmet in a plastic bag, and put it outside. Lice can't live without food for long, and they can't crawl out of the plastic. After a week or two, all the lice should be dead.

son was getting the lice from ONE batting helmet they all shared!

Lice can live only a day or two without food. If they drop off one person's head, they're in a big hurry to find another one. As soon as the lice find a good spot on the new head, they grab hold and begin to suck up blood. Soon after, the female lice start laying nits. After a while, some of the new adults fall off and find another new home. Then the cycle starts all over again.

Because lice move from one person to another so fast, it's tough to control them. That's why adults get so panicky. So if you think you might have lice, it's time to start a search.

Lice glue their nits to the base of a piece of hair.

On the Hunt for Lice

It's not always easy to tell if lice have invaded your school, but teachers are always on the lookout for them. Someone in your class might complain about an itchy head, or a teacher might see a kid scratching. For adults, that's a lice red alert!

First, they might ask all the kids—including you—if they have itchy heads. Teachers might also ask if anyone has shared a hairbrush, a comb, a hat, or a pillow. Then everyone will most likely get a head check.

Sharing a brush or a comb can spread head lice.

Having your head checked for lice doesn't hurt at all. The worst part is sitting still while the grown-up looks at your head—but you can do it!

First, your teacher or school nurse might ask you to sit or stand under a bright light. The light makes it easier to see nits. Then the adult will probably check the hair behind your ears and at the back of your neck. Those are a louse's favorite hiding places.

Next, the teacher will part your hair and look closely at your scalp. The teacher is looking for white nits. Lice usually lay their nits very close to the scalp.

If something looks like a nit, the teacher will try to scrape it off your hair with a fingernail. If it comes off easily, it's not a nit. It might be dandruff, flakes of skin, or flecks of hair spray. If it's stuck to your hair like superglue, it is probably a nit. Your head may be a lice hotel.

If your teacher finds lice or nits on just one person, the school will probably jump into action. Lice spread fast. It's important for everyone to be prepared. Many schools ask all the kids to take a note home. The note tells parents that lice have been found at school.

Your mom or dad might be very upset to get this note. Your parents

NO LICE

22

volun-
gener
worse,
much
mmo-
un-
at se-
and
eases
s that
great-
hock:
orsen
must
possi-
cycle.
lated
to re-
sula-
ation
oats,
pa-
with
lders
man
reeze
has
rosty

of the hole? The answer is that, field. How to read all E&S con-
without training, equipment, and trol plan and what to look for

I Had Lice and Survived!
A Second-Grader Tells Her Story

What is it like to have these creepy crawlies on your head? Alison Clark, a 7-year-old who lives in Honesdale, Pennsylvania, knows exactly how it feels. Here's her story.

"It was Halloween and Mom was combing my hair. She saw little white things running across my head—lice! We had to go shopping to look for lice shampoo on Thanksgiving. When we got home we shampooed and shampooed. It smelled awful.

"Then Mom got lice too! She was shampooing and shampooing her own hair. The next day I went to school. There was a long line at the nurse's office. She was check-ing everyone for head lice. My friend and I both had them. I guess the shampoo didn't kill them all.

"The nurse told me to go to class, but said not to get too close to anyone. I could feel the lice on my head. It felt like little raindrops falling on my head. It was very itchy. Every 5 seconds I was itching my head to death.

"At day care that day my friend and I got to stay in the back room all by ourselves. We played Nintendo for 2 hours. When I went home, Mom shampooed my head again. A little later, she checked my head and the lice were all gone. She was so happy!"

won't be mad at you, though. They might feel embar-
rassed. Some people think only dirty people catch
head lice, but that's not true.

Activity 2: Looking at a Louse

Lice can be neat to look at. Your teacher might have a microscope. Ask if you can put a nit or a live louse under it and take a look. Nits look like teardrop-shaped pouches stuck to hair strands. If a nit is about to hatch, you might see a tiny nymph inside. The nymph will probably look clear because it hasn't had its first meal of blood yet. If you have an adult louse, check out those claws! That's what it uses to hang onto your hair.

Head Lice or Body Lice?

Head lice don't care how clean or how dirty you are. All they care about is getting a meal. Body lice are different. They like it when someone doesn't take a bath very often. And they really like it when a person wears the same crusty clothes for weeks.

Body lice don't live on a person's skin. They live in clothes. When they get hungry, they jump on a person and take a bite.

Many years ago, when people didn't bathe as often, body lice were more common. Today it's unusual for someone in the United States to have body lice. But old ideas die hard. That's why some people think "dirty" and "gross" when they hear that someone has lice—even when it's head lice.

Head lice and body lice look alike, and they both eat human blood. So how are these two insects different?

Body lice are bigger, and they live in the folds and seams of clothes. When body lice get hungry, they crawl to the skin, have a quick bite, and crawl back into their warm fabric homes. Body lice can carry germs that cause diseases. When a body louse bites a person, it **transmits**, or passes on or spreads, the disease to the person. Head lice may be annoying, but they don't carry germs that cause disease.

Did You Know...

Has anyone ever said you have cooties? The word "cootie" is a nickname for body lice. It was first used during World War I, when lots of soldiers had body lice.

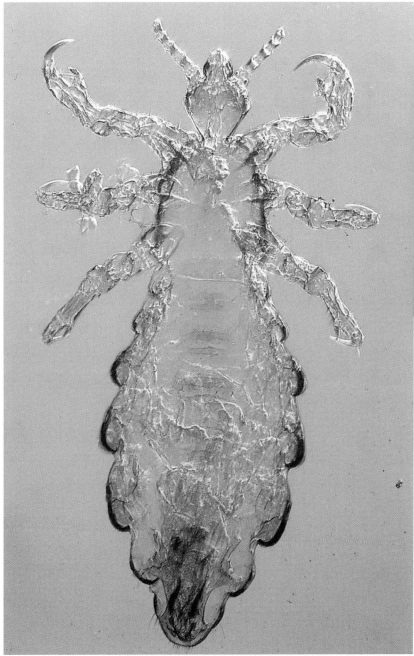

A body louse (left) looks a lot like a head louse (above), but only a body louse can make you sick.

Can Lice Be Stopped?

Waging war on head lice usually involves two steps. First, an adult must carefully check your head for lice and nits. This takes time, but picking them out by hand is the best way to get rid of the critters.

Before you begin Step 1 of your battle against lice, you'll need a few weapons.

- A patient adult. Removing lice takes time.
- A patient kid. That's YOU.
- A nit comb. This is a special metal comb. It's made to comb out the nits in your hair. Most lice shampoos come with a nit comb.
- Good lighting. Put a chair near a sunny window or under a bright lamp.
- A magnifying glass. Some lice and nits can be hard to see.
- A dry towel.
- Tweezers or double-sided tape. You'll find out more about this later.
- A cool videotape you haven't seen yet. This will help you sit still.

When you've gathered everything, you're ready to begin the battle. Let the patient adult comb your hair with a regular comb to get out all the tangles. Then wrap the dry towel around your shoulders, pop in that videotape, and get ready to sit still for an hour or two.

While you're watching the movie, your patient adult will divide your hair into sections and use the nit comb to inspect each section separately. The adult will begin

at your scalp and finish at the ends of your hair. If the comb gets full of lice or nits, the adult can dip the comb in a glass of water to clean it. If the nits are stuck on tight, your patient adult will use a fingernail to scrape them off. If the nits can't be scraped off, the adult can snip off the hair strand with a pair of scissors. Don't worry, no one will notice a few strands of hair missing.

Before moving to a second section, the adult will examine the first section one more time. There may be some nits that didn't come off the first time. By the time your patient adult has checked all the sections, the movie will probably be almost over.

Now its time to look for adult lice. They move fast, so this is where the magnifying glass comes in handy. Lice can be caught with the tweezers or stuck with the double-sided tape. By now, the movie should be over and all the lice should be gone!

NO VACANCY

Tweezers are good for nabbing any stray louse that thinks it might escape.

Even after all this work, lice sometimes come back. Maybe your patient adult missed a nit or two. Maybe you'll get new lice from a friend. It's a good idea for an adult to check your head every day for a week or so.

If more nits show up, the adult should remove them with a comb or a fingernail. If the adult finds three or four new nits every day, it's time for Step 2—washing your hair with a special lice shampoo. Lice shampoos

31

contain chemicals that kill lice. This is a little different from everyday hair washing. You need an adult to do it for you. It's important to follow the instructions on the shampoo bottle carefully.

After the shampoo, your patient adult will probably want to check your head again. The lice have been beaten. Time to relax. Right? Well . . . the war isn't over yet. Now you've got to defend yourself against another

You might have to wash your hair a few times with the lice shampoo before all the lice are gone.

Don't Try This at Home

Arrg! The lice just won't go away. Will anything get rid of these pests? You might hear about a home remedy that works. Check with an adult before you slop any weird goo on your head. Most home remedies are harmless. But some can be down-right dangerous.

- Vinegar. Some people think that a mixture of vinegar and water loosens the gummy substance that holds nits onto the hair, but all it really does is make your hair smell like salad dressing.
- Lard, Vaseline, or cooking oil. They might suffocate some of the adult lice, but they probably won't get rid of the nits.
- Kerosene or gasoline. Never try this home remedy. These liquids may kill lice, but they could hurt you too. Kerosene and gasoline are **flammable** liquids they catch on fire easily.
- Pet shampoos. The chemicals in these shampoos are safe for your pets, but some can be harmful to people. And do you really want to smell like a clean dog?
- Hair coloring. This may give the lice new colors to look at, but it won't get rid of them.
- A short haircut. Your new look might be cool, but lice like short hair just as much as long hair. If you want to shave your head, that's different. That will get rid of the lice.
- Lawn and garden chemicals. These substances may kill lice, but they could also hurt you.

attack. There are a few things you and your family can do to help keep the lice from moving back in.

The biggest job in your house will most likely be the cleaning. Hats, scarves, and any other clothes that might have been on your head should be washed. All your bedding—sheets, blankets, pillowcases, everything—should go into the washing machine and the dryer. The heat of the dryer is what

Most lice can't survive a ride in a hot dryer.

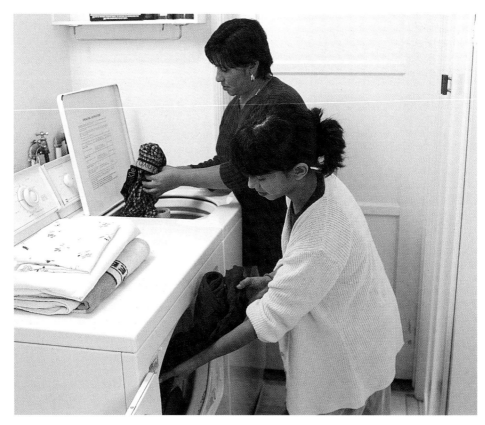

After the house is vacuumed, remember to empty the vacuum bag. Any lice that survive could crawl back out again.

really kills the lice. Check labels to make sure that it's safe to stuff your stuff in the dryer.

You should also put your stuffed toys in plastic bags and leave them outside for a week or so. Any lice on them will starve to death. It's a good idea to vacuum rugs, backs of chairs, furniture, car seats, headrests, and anything else that comes in contact with people's heads.

All the combs and brushes in the house need a good cleaning, too. Some people soak their brushes and combs in hot water or lice shampoo. Other people just throw them out and buy new ones.

All this hard work will be wasted if someone brings lice in from somewhere else. Everyone in your house should get a head check each day for a week or so. If no one gets lice again, you can declare your house a Lice-Free Zone.

When your head lice are gone, it's time to go back to school. What happens at school during a lice attack? What can you expect when you go back? Keep reading to find out.

School Versus Lice: Who Will Win?

Lice spread fast in school. Teachers know this, so even if only one child has lice, your teachers will want to check everybody. The school nurse or another health person may help out. You might get out of class to stand in line for a headcheck. Watching the adults dig through everyone's hair can be a funny sight!

If the adults find anyone else with lice, they may separate that person from the rest of the class. If there are lice on your head, they might make you sit or stand by yourself for a while. Don't feel bad. You didn't do anything wrong. They just want to make sure that the lice don't spread to other people.

Did You Know...

Millions of people in the United States get head lice every year. Most of them are kids younger than 12 years old.

While some teachers are checking heads, others might start separating everyone's coats and hats. If someone in your classroom has lice, your teacher might put that person's stuff in a plastic bag. You might also see the teachers vacuuming and cleaning.

Garbage bags are perfect for storing toys, pillows, and other things that might have lice on them. The bags should be closed tightly to keep any lice from crawling out.

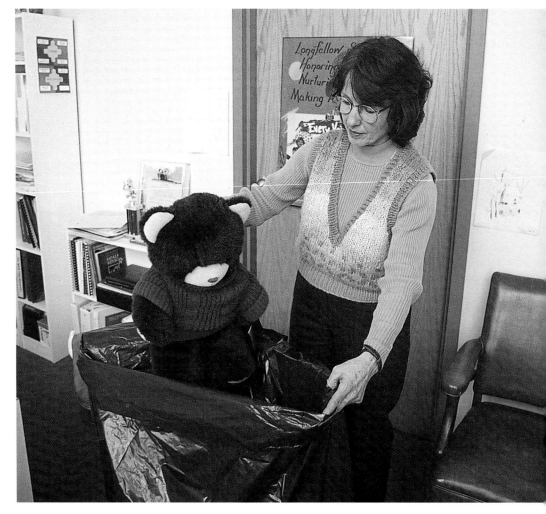

Parents sometimes get very upset when head lice turn up at a school. Some adults don't understand that head lice are really harmless. Others might think the school is a dirty place.

Many teachers know how upset parents can get. They want to make parents feel better, so they make rules about lice. Some schools have a "no nit" rule. That means anyone who has nits can't come to school.

If you have lice, get ready for a vacation from school. But don't get too excited. Getting rid of all the nits might not take more than a day.

There may be new rules about what you can wear to school.

Did You Know...

Nitpicky people pay too much attention to details. That saying got started a long time ago. Back then, the only way to get rid of lice was to carefully remove all the nits by hand. So nitpicky people had to pay close attention to what they were doing!

Keep your own hat on when you play sports. That way you won't get lice from someone else's cap!

You may not be able to wear your favorite hat anymore. Sports helmets might go on the "don't wear" list, too. Teachers might ask you not to bring combs or brushes to school.

Some of these rules may seem silly. But if schools don't have rules, it might take months to get rid of all the lice. No one wants to scratch that long!

Lice Aren't So Bad!

Lice can be a pain to deal with. They might make you miss school. They might make your family turn your house upside down. Your favorite sweater might shrink to doll-size in the dryer. You'll probably never wash your hair so much again!

The worst part of having lice is how you feel when you get them. It's embarrassing, and maybe a little scary. The thought of having creepy crawlies on your head is nasty!

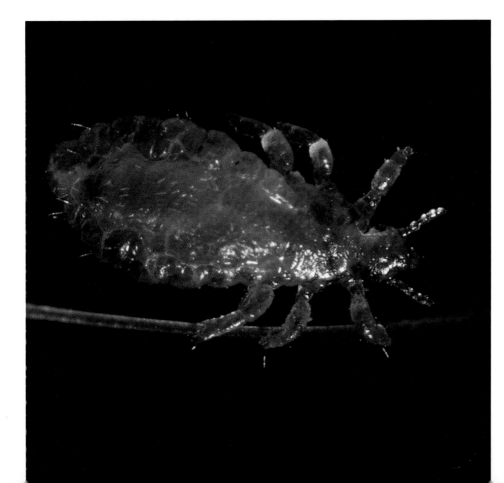

Head lice like the hair at the back of your head and behind your ears the best.

But head lice aren't monsters. They're just insects, like butterflies or ladybugs. All they're looking for is a place to live and a warm meal. They can't help it if their favorite place to live is on a human head.

Something about these little critters makes people very nervous. But they aren't really gross. We just think they are. And as long as we do, we'll keep going nuts whenever they appear.

Sometimes head lice lay their nits on eyelashes.

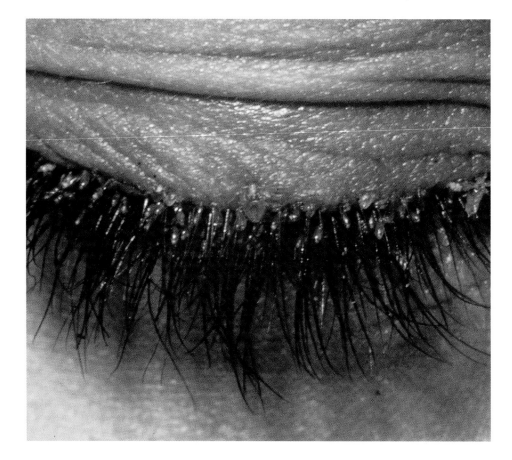

Glossary

ectoparasite—a creature that lives and feeds on the out-side of another living thing

exoskeleton—the hard outer covering of insects, lobsters, shrimp, and some other animals without a backbone

flammable—catches on fire easily

nymph—the young of a louse

nit—a louse egg

parasite—a creature that lives and feeds on another living thing

transmit—to pass on or spread

Learning More

Books

Cottam, Clarence. *Insects: A Golden Guide*. Racine, WI: Western Publishing Co., 1987.

Leahy, Christopher. *Peterson's First Guide to Insects*. Boston: Houghton Mifflin, 1987.

Rice, Judith, Julie Stricklin, and Petronella J. Ytsma. *Those Itsy-Bitsy Teeny-Tiny Not-So-Nice Head Lice*. New York: Red Leaf Press, 1998.

Organizations and Online Sites

Baltimore County Department of Health Fact Sheet
http://www.co.ba.md.us/bacoweb/services/health/html/hdlice.htm
Learn more about how to identify and treat head lice.

Frequently-Asked Questions About Headlice
http://www.ces.ncsu/edu/depts/ent/notes/Urban/lice/lice-faq.htm
Find answers to all your questions about head lice.

National Pediculosis Association
P.O. Box 149
Newton, MA 02161

Health Education Center
Lenox Hill Hospital
Park Avenue at 77th St.
New York, NY 10028

Safe Control of Head Lice
http://www.crisny.org/not-for-profit/nycap/headlice.htm
This site features useful diagrams of the head louse life cycle
and the parts of a nit as well as information about head lice.

Welcome to Headlice.org
http://www.headlice.org/index.html
Get the latest news about head lice and read ten steps to help
keep your hair free of lice and nits.

Index

About the Author

Allison Lassieur studied writing and journalism at the University of Central Arkansas. She enjoys writing about animals, science, and history—the grosser the better. She has published two books about history, *Life in a Medieval Castle* and *Before the Storm*, which is about Native American life. When Ms. Lassieur isn't at her computer in her office in Quakertown, Pennsylvania, she likes traveling, reading, and making medieval costumes.